Objects in the Terrifying Tense
Longing from Taking Place

T0308018

For my parents,
Dee Scalapino and Robert Anthony Scalapino

Objects in the Terrifying Tense
Longing from Taking Place

Leslie Scalapino

ROOF BOOKS

NEW YORK

ISBN: 0-937804-54-1
Library of Congress Catalog Card No.: 94-065017

Acknowledgments: an earlier version of "Thinking Serially" was published in *Talisman*; "One Grasps the Implications of This Negative as a Whole" was published in *Aerial*; passages from "Objects in the Terrifying Tense" were published in *Conjunctions* and *Leaves*. The chapter, *From: The Front Matter, Dead Souls*, is from a novel by the same title written by Leslie Scalapino. Quotes from, *The Collected Poems of Robert Creeley, 1945-1975*: Copyright 1983 The regents of the University of California. Reprinted by permission of the University of California Press.

The title of this book is a line from *Metamorphopsia* by Norma Cole.

The author is grateful to Robert Grenier for his close reading and comments on the manuscript of this text bringing attention to elements that needed change and rewriting.

This book was made possible, in part, by a grant from the New York State Council on the Arts and the National Endowment for the Arts.

Roof Books
are published by
Segue Foundation
303 East 8th Street
New York, NY 10009

Chapters

Introduction

My intention in *Objects in the Terrifying Tense / Longing from Taking Place* is to juxtapose shapes of various contemporary works of writing in a resemblance of their own structures to 'real' events (which these writings as if floating in reciprocal shapes are as much as are occurrences in the world) to see their real occurrence in the present.

My premise, which is rendered cumulatively in the whole of the book as one work, is stated in the final chapter: "What's modern is the writing being to state structure in order to see 'objectively' its reverberation solely."

The intention in the following is to allow the shapes of the structures of the texts being considered to emerge. These texts' characteristic is in stating their own structures as their forms which is *per se* scrutiny of the present.

If the writing is on ('seeing') something that's real, it keeps disappearing as the occurrence, as the occurrence does. The comparison of the image to the living object is occurrence as rim of observation, in the comparison of these texts. One is seeing their observation of the object, as an image, to see.

In the reality which is created by a writing, to narrow to the outlines of its form is utter scrutiny, is real. It's the interior relation of experience.

The proximity of events in it as such is place and change, which I want to see here without subjecting it to my writing.

This is making a 'first' shape, trying to see their shapes without it.

The allowance in this writing only of 'relation' is the interiority, which is the sole narrative.

An H.D. Book

The description, and undercutting, of war (World War II) as "An incident here and there" is in relation to the tiny self. We're overwhelmed: for the small poem to be a palimpsest.

If ruin opens in the past, in the papyrus, history, the dream, as it does in the present, what's a dream one has?

Is the grass mast by jewelled mast of nature the dream? Is the dream which is projected from oneself the limitless with the flying worm of oneself in it traveling and eating, tiny.

It's circular. So the worm can't be destroyed. But the worm must be able to be destroyed in the writing: which must have 'the real actions of/in the world' (what we experience as real), with oneself, together.

One would be destroyed by the writing being that of only those 'actions in the world', no other existing. The converse is to allow for the small self in continual imbalance: in which the 'world' is part of and 'within' the defenseless self.

H.D. allows the imbalance: a sense of an infinite structure of possible actions that is the world overwhelming the tiny self: is the *form* of the writing.

Thought "states economically / in a simple dream-equation" statement of relations. The relations between things, the structure, is the belief that there can be any 'relation' of it.

Yet if ruin opens in the past, as it does now, one has to

be fragile as a means to see structure in that the worm is peculiarly free.

One's minute movements in the writing don't mimic reality but rather appear with reality, as part of it.

H.D.'s structure (of belief and in writing) is that there are relations which can be posited, but only as the means of seeing, having a way to describe, occurrence. Occurrence is real and not visible to us ever.

(These thoughts on H.D. mimic the structure and intention of my text, *Objects in the Terrifying Tense, Longing from Taking Place*. Actions in reality, as if at the same time, appear as the formal shapes in current writing.

The thoughts of my text don't mirror literary criticism, are shapes of writing, are their present. Viewing by scrutiny, and elimination of all of the individual parts, illuminates the whole.)

One's small, static, limited, so the base is "self-out-of-self." One is closed and so "selfless, /that pearl-of-great-price."

> Bitter, bitter jewel
> in the heart of the bowl

One's interior's feeding into a duality of the structure (of the world) and oneself. Occurrence isn't either. Occurrence is the jewel, oneself's the jewel.

H.D. presses two lines together merging throughout the three-part series (*Trilogy*) so that merging they're not subject to war.

The self is so small and beautiful, whole, that it can't merge. Its own inner rim compares to its rim.

> a worm on the leaf,
> a worm in the dust,

The dual worm-cycle is in language intrinsically. The world/oneself/nature are enmeshed, three here paired as if dual. They can't be thus paired.

So the possible 'infinite' compressed comparisons which are the relations, perceived by the viewer/oneself, are relativistic (Einsteinian), merely markers.

When the 'self' or what's thought of as that merges peacefully there's no separation of there (in the structure) from existence (no comparison to it).

The bitter jewel is empty peacefully in the structure.

That tears apart what is now as it has no 'relation' possible. Narrative solely has to change seeing.

Other cultures are consumed and are the present. All images arise on that. We float off that.

Cultures are relativistic and torn apart by 'our existence now' being compared to (such as) the actual dawn sky 'only'; our sense of reality is myriads of comparisons *per se*, pairs. Now is vast negative in its own rim implied.

Writing has to not produce that, what's our culture now, which is then not producing in being calm. That's the worm being able to be destroyed. We are seeing the images we create now which is seeing (our) history.

On *Helen in Egypt*

The place (the outside) is change *per se*. It is the light elation, a state of dreaming that is awake.

Writing in its simplest movement is the light elation. The movements are only in that and induce themselves.

(Alternately described in *Helen in Eygpt* as trance, dream, waking dream, non-remembrance, "ecstatic or semi-trance state" which is "suppressed memory", gives way to, or always is, the waking lightly lucid state from which reading of history/and the self and the secretion, myth, occurs. "I am awake, I see things clearly; it is dawn" is waking dream or day-dream. "Numb with memory" is being in history, which is illusion, and being the secretion as myth, which is illusion. The waking dream and being "numb with memory"are the same:

The pictures are read according to "phases" or "mood", even "formula", and subject to "new enchantment", which are the changes of observation itself as their scrutiny. It is subject to itself only.)

H.D. wrote only in that level, never left it (in *Helen in Eygpt*). The statement of relations is *per se* the actions of Eros, Achilles as meeting, or Helen as the thousand-petalled lily the self, by their having no other occurrence except as their delineation.

Myth is an illusion that is the light elation.

Maintaining that imbalance infinitely is the worm.

The delineations (reading hieroglyphs as pictures on the wall), which are the minute movements of the writing, don't mimic reality, but appear with reality:

Maintaining the imbalance and the separate delineation is the utter illusion and transience of one.

The text, as well as the structure of the text, is the "One finite moment" in which the one is in utter illusion (as the heroic moment of Achilles) "to break one's heart for a memory forgotten." This undercuts and renders illusory the structure and the basis of the text (and of existence) while at the same time, awake, adhering to its illusion as the sole scrutiny.

By inducing change as incremental only and not causal the entire structure which causes nothing is changed throughout. It is not even the light elation, while being that itself.

It occurs in the shape and sound in the line breaks throughout retroactively, later when the entire illusion of the structure is only the light elation which is not founded in one.

The text/the dream is a "timeless dimension" in which "Time values have altered, present is past, past is future."

Helen's lover Paris is later her son; Helen in one phase of

"non-remembrance" is Thetis, Achilles' mother, at the same time as meeting him in Eygpt (Leuké, also La Mort, L'Amor) for the first time. At times all projections are one, the self, which are maintained separate; these are the form of the structure itself:

> Proteus enchanted me,
> he disclosed the mystery
> when they reach a certain degree,
>
> they are one, alike utterly

H.D.'s nerve was to openly base the structure on illusion made precarious by the apparent base of the self (thus *it* is illusory). Seeing the psyche as structure as myth/as illusion, the incremental structure is set free.

Trilogy, H.D., New Directions, New York,1973
Helen in Eygpt, New Directions, New York, 1974

Extinction of Images

Extinction of images in Danielle Collobert's writing ("on the outskirts of calm / extinction of images") to get to the place where there is no identity is the place of actual identity unmediated by discursive reasoning or language which constitutes a divorce from self which is the real (that is, the place of no identity as body and as writing: "the imaginary written absolute . . . . no identity of any kind anywhere in the dust").

Yet the writing is to dream up a place where identity happens, which is the body itself: "a container of identity / body skull the head — to keep to these solid limits against / the fluidity — the fear of not being its words / a place then — to dream up a place where identity happens").

Anguish or pain are merely negative space freeing being, by the recognition of the inherent destitution of the being; akin to the eye gazing at itself and seeing nothing there.

> imaginary capture
> to say to itself
> to the eye its gaze
> turns the glove of anguish inside out
> destitution of the being

"Extinction of images" is 'not continuing' the chain of images which constitutes being, and writing. The writing is unfinished phrases connected by dashes, devoid, "Like dead the buried text."

This state of extinction of images is "still motion"; yet she doesn't reach it, continually: "the motionless never."

The effort is the "hopeless waiting to touch being." Touching actual being entails mutilation of the constructed self ("to undo itself in the amputation of the words"), the writing actually being dead moments; it is causing a "fixity of dead moments." It is 'active' negatively in that sense, so the dead moments are also lost, extinguished while being present. The enactments of the body are repeated as "waste products" which are sloughed off.

The "wordless body," absence of voice, speech, hearing, which are forms of discursive distinction, is delineated as a state of empty 'bliss'. It "seeks its night" in "waves of red, without order, without distinction."

In *Zen* practice 'appearances' which *are* the world are the same as mind. The mind is freed from itself and those appearances by delusion itself. It can only *be* in delusion.

Collobert's effort is to create a state of painless bliss where the chain of creation ceases: "no longer fit together the scraps / off the track — chains of opaque." Insofar as Collobert's writing gesture is the mutilation of the self, it imagines a self, which is not akin to *Zen*. She who ended her own life at the age of thirty-eight was practicing writing as a literal experiment to be at the very line of flesh and consciousness, so it is where flesh and writing are to be the same.

Her 'myth', so to speak, was of the existence of the flesh and mind as entity and so wanting to do away with it. Her writing is not romantic in the sense of ego, or posturing of the self in relation to the writing. The body and writing are object(ive).

One is being the edge of flesh not existing always, and therefore doesn't need to create that.

There is no society, only the flesh as if an eye reflecting its own process. Society is narrowed to be the present self striving for extinction.

Flesh and edge of flesh existing, and not existing, and edge of the writing (articulated as its subject, itself — as the actual flesh — being the notation or observation of it) produce each other.

The observation of the flesh is to be melded to be it.

One's flesh not being known as being is discursive reasoning.

Collobert's writing functionally 'being' the characteristics of flesh, those characteristics do not maintain, or even observe, society. They are not produced by society.

The writer is pushed in the writing to being isolated in being born. What's prior is at the same time. No one (else) is there, really no one at all. Writing is a method of seeing by the flesh not *ever* seeing, and being in existence. The writing therefore doesn't have mythic faculties. These are *per se* of society, not in observation itself.

Mythic faculties exist in Collobert's construct only as desire for an "imaginary written absolute" which would be "no identity": myth is 'society's fantasy'. To erase the notion of paradise inherent in societies is the edge of phenomena not being produced by our society.

One's flesh as being is unknown to one. So the dichotomy between critical/discursive reasoning/or language, and that which is poetic writing, is about itself. Collobert was fracturing that schism to omit reflection of social order. Her delusion doesn't have birds flying and so the phenomenal world collapses.

Traditions, such as the Troubadors' songs do exist, float freely regardless of time as indications that one has to see. Form is instructions for, knowledge of the way of seeing, yet it is of a particular circumstance, location: what it sees *is* it. No rules or social caste determine seeing if it's occurring.

Collobert writes outside of confinement of traditions as caste, maybe having to extinguish 'oneself' to do that.

Yet no one can extinguish 'oneself', in the sense of being weighted by traditions, to see the real, which is only the present.

(*It Then*, Danielle Collobert, translated by Norma Cole, O Books, Oakland, 1989)

'Thinking Serially' in *For Love*, *Words* and *Pieces*

The social conditions in which the courtly love poem arose were such that relations between people are convention. If one is looking at relations between people in their writing, that is convention — as the writing's form.

Creeley uses the form as inherent conflict by its being (only) present time.

His particular circumstance or place (in the poem), the factor of being in it, does not allow convention. 'One's' only existence is in conflict *per se*. The being of 'one' is conflict. He sees the real as only the present.

Poems in *For Love* use the convention of Elizabethan love poem or quality of medieval courtly love tradition, written as Creeley's present time: as that is what is actually occurring (in the conception of marriage; or the courtly conception of the idealized love, which is outside of marriage) — the two continually separate. *For Love* is a serial work because it is inherently conflict which starts again and again: it has the quality of being precisely that which is its form; so the 'theme' of the poems is its form.

> Moving in the mind's
> patterns, recognized
> because there is where
> they happen. [1]

Creeley's 'two' who are separate are sometimes the lover

and his lady, or two ladies, one in the lover's mind and one in reality; or the lover himself who is double split internally as being both the lady and himself.

> I know two women
> and the one
> is tangible substance,
> flesh and bone.
>
> The other in my mind
> occurs.
> She keeps her strict
> proportion there ("The Wife," CP 252

Delineation of the conflict is the form of the poem.

> In the dream
> I see
> two faces turned,
>
> one of which
> I assume mine, one
> of which I assume
>
> . . . .
> If all women are
> mothers, what
> are men
>
> standing
> in dreams, mine
> or theirs,
>
> empty of
> all but themselves.
> They are so
> lonely, unknown
> there, I run

for whatever

is not
them, turning
into that consequence

makes me
my mother hating
myself. ("The Dream," CP 298)

The only description is the weight of the measure itself, the tracking that is the poem. The poem is serial because it is separate, because it is its measure. The poems are a series because they are separate and continuous. There may be a reversal of what's actually being said, the form of experience:

I will never get there.
Oh Lady, remember me
who in Your service grows older
not wiser, no more than before.

How can I die alone.
Where will I be then who am now alone,
what groans so pathetically
in this room where I am alone?
    ("The Doors," CP 201)

Position in ordering (from the reader's perspective, or writer's, of the serial collection) is arbitrary; perspective is no ordering. "Position is where you / put it, where it is" ("Window," CP 284). That's why he would die alone: the shapes that one creates do not mimic reality, but appear with reality, are part of it. One can't be united with one. (I'm reading *For Love, Words,* and *Pieces* as chronological collection, not considering these as separate 'books.')

If perspective is no ordering, the chronologically ordered *Collected* is a range and configuration of potential, infinite actions which are on the edge-of-seeing their actual occurring (by *being* chronological). The shape and movement of the real past event — which was as that time's present — is activated in configurations continuously.

The senses recreate the particular place which is then closure of that place ("Variations," CP 288). The individual component of the series is not description ("I do not feel / what it was I was feeling"); and therefore the 'place' does not exist once it is over and the writing must begin again. Unlike the courtly love poem, serial thinking is what Creeley's poem is beginning in *For Love*. It's articulated as the 'two' which are separate, and a series: "in its feeling, / two things, / one and one" ("Song," CP 319). (I'm considering the numbers 'two.' A series of numbers, moving the center off 'two,' occurs in *Pieces*.)

The terms that courtly love convention posits are that one's being is possible only within those courtly terms: in impossible union. For Creeley, one can never equal one. Being absolutely in the present and absolutely separate from it at the same time:

THE WINDOW

> There will be no simple
> way to avoid what
> confronts me. Again and
> again I know it, but
> take heart, hopefully,
> in the world unavoidably
> present. Here, I think,
> is a day, not a
> but the. My hands are
>
> shaking, there is
> an insistent tremble
> from the night's
> drinking. But what

15

was I after, you
were surely open to me.
Out the far window
there was such intensity

of yellow light. But love,
love I so wanted I
got, didn't I, and then
fell senseless, with relief. (CP 336)

The mystery of that being (it being that form) is union.
The union isn't the love.

It's a space or 'inner' configuration that's unknown and to which the love is articulated.

Creeley's writing in these works is in continual conflict between an overriding conception, and the process which is being within the series and not seeing what's ahead: "is an event only / for the observer? / No one / there" (CP 379). Creeley, in *Pieces*, is moving around in what he characterizes as an American quality of event or mind: having no over-riding conception, continually resisting such, which itself creates it.

Americans have a funny way —
somebody wrote a poem about it —
of "doing nothing" — What else
should, can, they do?

✿

What
by being not
is — is not
by being. (CP 406)

That hole ("When holes taste good / we'll put them in our bread") is merely a component of that place (of or in the series). The theme of hole or circle, sometimes delineating seeing only

16

within the mind's own forms repetitively, or an emptiness (*not* repetitive) that is joy (*Words*: "The Circle," CP 343; "The Hole," CP 344; "Joy," CP 350) is only the particular articulation of those spaces there (in the series) as the number zero.

The fixed place or the place which is recreated by the senses and thus closed, is the point of being separated from the present. It is where: *They* were imagination, and the *world* also; the rules known prior to be wrong — then the mind followed and I also as it was true. Phenomena has to be ahead of mind. It is the 'ground of people,' the place or relation between people as the form of the writing, the converse of definition *by* place (as in "The Puritan Ethos," CP 414, the geographical mind space which displaces the "other space" that is "several / dimensional locus").

The "several dimensioned locus" is the serial work that is really all over, multiple. It occurs in the ground that has been excluded by the conception of 'higher authority'/Puritan Ethos (our *actual* social construction) for which work, the visible result and activity, *not* the relationship between people, exists. These 'relations' as such (as *private* mind) aren't hierarchical, except when interpreted through convention of that hierarchy. So they don't exist except outside it.

If erotic love is knowledge to be tracted occurrence isn't ever seen.

As in the courtly love tradition, the dual consciousness of the 'Puritan heritage' is to be transcended. The autobiography, the 'life', in this society is to be obliterated. The 'confessional self' of writing is a format, so it obliterates the 'real.' Creeley is obliterating literary 'confessional self' by the 'life' being.

In the poem "The Window," 'reaching' (or being in) love is being in *the* day, the unavoidable single present world. If "They"/American/or Puritan Ethos are imagination and the *world* also, they are constituting a geographical mind space that excludes the possibility of that relation with people (i.e., that of

17

being in the unavoidable single present *world*).

The American's funny way of "doing nothing" is such being in the single present world. The "several dimensioned locus" of the serial writing is not planned, or composed which is ordered in advance. The components/individual poems of the 'series' (the three works read as chronological collection) are delineations of that mind space of that particular poem as it occurs.[2] In-so-far as a poem delineates the conflict of 'convention'/of 'love,' for example, the poem is literally the presentation of the "mind's patterns" rather than a hierarchical imposition on that mind space substituting social convention as the point of view ("The Dream," CP 298). Poems in For *Love* and *Words* using courtly love conventions/as reflection of American/or Puritan Ethos space, as serial thinking are "doing nothing" in the sense of being in the single present world only where that very *convention*/of love is not taking place. (Creeley's intention is not to be in convention.)

The mind's patterns contain convention and repeat it but do not remain in it in the serial writing, though it is a race to continually move off of the dead center which is its formation:

> Quicker
> than that, can't
> get off "the
> dead center of"
>
> myself. He/I
> were walking. Then
> the place is/was
> not ever enough. ("A Sight," CP 340)

The mind space that is 'created' which is the form of these poems is the geographical space of that love; where one is most oneself, and thus alone in the heretical sense/of our Puritan Ethos.

It is actually where relationship between people can occur, heretical for that reason; in that that specificity is the *world* ("The Providence," CP 415) unraveled from 'that' mind imposition.

It is ahead of the dissolution of the self as 'real.'

The form of the *Collected* can be a being in 'history' by virtue of its ground/the individual poem (i.e., the particular configuration/form of a conflict as a component in a series of such) *not* mirroring that which is outside. It is to be the opening of a space (that of American "doing nothing") which is what is really outside — i.e., outside of the mind's continual imposition of the/its own form. Resisting one's / and *their* ("They," CP 417) 'formation' I think is the meaning of Creeley's comment:

> I've always been embarrassed for a so-called
> larger view. I've been given to write about that
> which has the most intimate presence for me . . . I
> think, for myself at least, the world is most evident
> and most intense in those relationships. Therefore
> they are the materials out of which my work is made.
> (Contexts 97)

Creeley's use of autobiographical reference, is following the movement of itself in time (watching the mind) — rather than the expression of 'creation' of a personality. Its mirroring of its own mind formation and its race to out-run that as 'serial thinking' is not static personality creation *because* it is only that movement.

This internally produced 'argument' (the mind watching itself and trying to outrace its own closure, as a 'particular' form in this time) rather than being a trap that ultimately enshrines the self, are pieces in the collection of writing which by the very fact of occurring as 'merely' components repeating a conflict, as it shows up, *without* essential change, are not 'that' (fixed) psychology.

The central fear of the 'Puritan Ethos' is that which is "internally produced" — heretical precisely because it is the American "doing nothing," what Creeley identifies in Williams:

"He knew that you change your mind every time you see something, and — what is it he says? — 'A new world is only a new mind'. So the context is continually what you can feel and where you are" (*Contexts* 17).

The grounds for our elimination of eroticism (as the extension of the terms of Puritan heritage) is the contention that it is the area quintessentially subjective and egoistic; the assumption 'now' is even that eroticism itself is inherently sexist. That's what *social context* may reflect.

If eroticism is eliminated in the sense of not seeing it in or as being the occurrence, that leaves only that social context; there is then no area existing for apprehension or change. We are split from ourselves, and therefore are *not* articulated. This occurs as the conditions of writing then.

The corollary of the dual strand (of Puritan Ethos) is that subjectivity is regarded as inherently contaminated, not only because it is ego *per se*; but also because as such it becomes a literary commodity *either* as confessional writing *or* the process of the unraveling and examination of the personality as the writing's form.

H.D.'s bitter jewel/worm-cycle is seen as the self, which when the *world* allows only itself, isn't of the 'real.' Creeley's saying self is only being the 'real.'

Robert Wilson's form of theater presentation is many scenes unfolding beside or out of each other which therefore seemingly take place within a limitless context. The quality of it not being in a 'box' derives from it emanating from the viewer, by the viewer seeing it. Similarly, Creeley's *Collected* has the quality that 'you' are creating it.

Wilson's visual spectacle unfolding unmediated by language (in the unfolding not being formed seemingly by language — our impression is not 'informed' by it) creates a sense of sites/sights essentially not changed from their 'original.'

One/the viewer is seeing them and ordering them as a 'history'. Creeley's *Collected* maintains its 'original seeing' repeating it as oneself seeing it.

(1) Robert Creeley, *The Collected Poems* (Berkeley Univ. California Press, 1982), p. 437. cited hereafter in text. Robert Creeley, *The Collected Poems of Robert Creeley, 1945-1975*.
(2) Robert Creeley, *Contexts of Poetry: Interviews 1961-1971* (Bolinas, Ca: Four Seasons Foundation, 1973), p. 101. Cited hereafter in text.

One Grasps the Implications
of This Negative as a Whole

The inscription for *Decay* reads "Ever since I've been doomed to die / all the lines I've ever known in my / life are coming back to my mind. / It must be a sign of mental decay." They're extinguished.

In *Decay*, the visual scenes that take place in 'frames' or lines may be on top of each other or to the side — or as if they cross each other — and there isn't a romantic hero, because they cross each other.

The lines meet and in that way are eliminated, as if there's no field there. The field does not exist, that had been created by them.

Two

A & B are sitting on the truncated
pyramidal rim of a black asphalt highway.
In the distance to the right is a black
mountain w / silver-white snowstorm on top.
There is a rainbow over a deep open field.
Under a dark green tree, a funeral party
leaving the grave, an open black hole.

One doesn't have to elude (to) a 'romantic' image of oneself, whatever that is. It is the area of the most extreme falsity. 'One' should get to that which is 'real', as such single when it is (almost) eliminated.

'You' can only see them when they cross or coincide with each other.

Like "Two," the poem "XY" has two points throughout which eliminate each other. Similarly, in "Ice Skating" the lines, motions, and surfaces are double continually and eliminate the surface.

A single line in these poems is double (so the writer is 'almost' eliminated): "This week I sat in a small room and wondered constantly where I was. / It is a bodily experience to be left as an orphan crying at the gate."

This observation of what's occurring or seen places a line under heavy stress: "The lack of any backbone marked an early disinclination to speech." There's no equivalent as representation of what it's/he's saying. Nor of the real, visual scene.

"Looking at the clock, flesh singed and blackened by the mysterious air." The speaker is looking at the clock; and there is flesh, either his or other's, singed and blackened by the mysterious air. Seeing double, or singular, causes the 'images' to cross each other. Or their crossing each other causes them to be singular or double. There's no way in the writing to know which.

"Circular thinking arrests emotional development, punishing time." This eliminates development and the conception of time as accruing. Change occurs; one's nature, anyone's, does not develop.

Perhaps the person's nature itself is regarded as romantic, falsity? That would be a falsity.

"One man walking down a street will see no more than he desires." But we don't know if that limits him. The sources of apprehension are not where they appear, because "Memory is estranged." Being estranged is not alienation; there isn't that, which is an idea of 'the self suffering'. "Out of the endless listing of addresses, he saw a human being burning white."

Nor is apprehension determined by rearrangement of elements.

The writing is white because it is "unborn in the eye, without reason or heart." Rearrangement does not exist in this. Decay is the outer meeting the inner in that way.

To narrow to the outlines of its form is utter scrutiny, is real.

"Outside the inner man's almost doubled back." So there may be suffering but it appears as calm, produced by estrangement. "I remove my two arms and / start to walk again."

There being no development of one's nature the inner and outer are flattened. As a fact.

My nature seemed to develop. (One has the illusion that one's nature develops.) Not really if the lines that are written are all that I was able to remember.

The images can't develop. The images aren't my nature.

Conduit, Barrett Watten, Gaz Press, 1988

Watten's writing is lovely in engaging in rigor (in the sense in which scientists speak of an experiment being elegant in its form and execution). It's not on the edge, it's the edge.

"One grasps the implications of this negative as a whole."

Viewing by scrutiny, and elimination of all of the individual parts, illuminates the whole.

The original world which is wonderful is seen only by seeing its 'negative' aspect, which occurs by duplicating it as wonderful.

The pretext to represent the original world is itself negative. "The text will be as wonderful as the falling star of its original, the world."

The negative panes through which this is seen are 'accurate' indirectly because "Normal vision has distorted its reasoning."

Nothing is accurate. Experience opens reality, which is only the mind's perception of it: "I think experience is access to language only."

Watten proposes the criteria of experience is not the individual's relation to it. Alienation is an illusion. The very rigor of negative space itself when held as a concept of self is also illusion, "Romantic negativity, the avoidance of any conditions that compromise the subject leading to the subject's lyrical denial of itself."

Experience itself is only communication. The writer's displacement is a relation to the reader's displacement. Therefore it seems (to me) that the criteria of experience *is* the individual's relation to it only:

It is not any collective "death of the subject" that accounts for the subject's removal from the work. Rather, it is the very conditions of communication, without which reading or hearing cannot take place. The reader is implicated in the structure of the writer's displacement, and the effaced intentions of the work are the reader being taken into account.

Supposing relativity is existence itself, there can be no mythic order or original act. Watten's aesthetic has the rigor of Zen practice, the most radical thinking, but he interprets the criteria negatively as a value: "if 'existence' rather than any of its components is the site of a representation that can never be stated directly, 'existence' itself must be acknowledged to be on the verge of collapse."

In that case, it collapses in scrutiny.

If one is troubled by there not being an original act, and therefore no direct statement of any act, this is a form of romantic negativity?

'Believing in a concept of rigor in itself as being the basis of apprehension' — is not rigorous thinking.

Conversely: 'Holding no concept is rigor' — is a concept. We're to make existence itself collapse.

In Watten's conception the socially created 'reality' cancels

25

itself out in negative space, which is theory of relativity. The existence of an entity is impossible.

The absent image is infinitely duplicated as a pair or ghost to the existing place.

Undoing the accepted 'reality' is continual as it is constantly being reestablished. The conservative nature of society is continually contradicted in negative space by seeing the image itself eliminated.

Dreams are thinking; to think is oppression. Oppressive experience and a decision alternate back and forth.

Say Persephone goes down to hell. That is the 'pagan' harrowing of hell. She is allowed back to earth/the world to cause spring. The conception that it is 'not' that she is 'allowed' dismantles negative space itself.

If she does not fulfill the other side of the equation (which is that of being denied), negative space undoes 'reality' by not denying it, not creating a context for it's formation.

Negative space is not created; black robes are blowing.

The wind is after the motorcade has gone by. The black robes fill flapping like sails.

Some of our women, prodded into cattle chutes and harnessed with black robes so that they are veiled with no eyeholes, walk behind the motorcade.

There's no consistency in imagery anywhere in it though there appears to be in 'reality.' That's one or us.

There isn't an interior experience as a comparison to the starving people in real time.

There's no rim or bulb of sun on it.

That's not contained. Here, we're to 'understand' as sentiment, as if we were the recipients naively.

We think we can extinguish images, which is the very emergence of being extinguished.

The hyena floating to one with the infant in its mouth is

within their convention, is in itself negative space, not for its formation.

Oppressive experience is not created nor is decision and are narrowed to the rim of observation. The rim itself (the premise) is eliminated.

If there is no denial, there can't be oppressive experience in spring.

It is possible for dreams or thought not to form oppressive experience. Where one does not avoid any conditions that compromise oneself (the opposite of romantic negativity) is (the notion of 'one's') existence collapsing (as one's prior sense of what experience is). So one isn't determined by nor producing one's continued conditions then. The self *is* then without being separated from social life, "this negative as a whole."

Society could be without *one's* alienation as the basis of its existence.

Decay, Barrett Watten, This Press, Berkeley, 1979
Conduit, Barrett Watten, Gaz Press, San Francisco, 1988

From: The Front Matter, *Dead Souls*, a serial novel to be published in the newspaper

Dead Souls

(I sent an early version of this to six or so newspapers, though it wasn't published, during the election campaign.)

Lyrical horror is our "participation in democracy" at the level of violence of compulsory voting in El Salvador. Taken as an assertion, then, such lyricism no longer works even as a form of bondage between writers. — *Barrett Watten*

Invisible, not that they're not real, actions occur so that one's seeing has to change to be realistic.

These actions are constantly denied by those in them, though sometimes they are not denied and are corroborated exactly.

So that seeing on the rim one could be free one feels but must see actions on the rim with or as where we live. One links them diverging because that is how to see it.

Unable to walk, there's no way for them to get to work.

Infants don't need to be born.

The eye in the sky floats, liquid, blue.

Silent reading is inner so it is the company bureaucracy in that it is centralized appearing to be pervasive, though one is alone reading what's similar.

Even greed in the bureaucracy has sunk retentive not appearing to be a motive.

The deaths of infants of a hundred and seventy thousand maybe in the aftermath of the war is not shown while they force children to be born.

A child is born for delight as its condition. Take fragments of the present. They are not shreds as newspaper text already but modulations of fragments in one.

Extreme is subjective and so not visible in them.

On the edge of the flat, the figure fills the bright blue air.

One doesn't have to figure out writing.

The images do not reflect back. They are only themselves, which is not in relation to existence.

Yet that is existence everywhere. This is to isolate the shape or empty interior of some events real in time so their 'arbitrary' location to each other emerges to, whatever they are.

The hyenas swarming for scraps are seen on the news, they're the anchormen.

This is a serial written to be chapters printed in installments in the newspaper, like Dickens' novels. The reader of the newspaper sees in current time. An arbitrary present time image exists in time here. Mimicking here in writing isn't representation.

The leering of the president's weak mouth on a bulging torso is twisted on pinched haunches as he runs away.

He's going to shoot at them again just to renew his popularity for his reelection campaign.

Thinking is having our original inferior nature. Only sentimentality is communing here. One can't know anyone that way so it isn't communing either. We sentimentalize our killing by wearing yellow ribbons. Not conforming here is the worst mark, being worthy of violence, ridicule for not being valued.

When someone's going to die, so it's repressed in one so as
to be sentimental there, that's its occurrence

the one who's not going to die fights
hyenas. Scrutinizing is bathos.

So one just imagines that and it's one's life,
the 'groundless' scrutiny.

Writing is only to be public.
Having deities at all mirrors their government.
The ghouls standing in a crowd crying for infants to be born,
their infants are free whether they're born or don't emerge there.

A patrician (in) seeing himself as such hangs onto a sense of
self (any sense of self is falsity *per se*).
Use a logic which is dissimilar to one's context (unknown to
it) to counter it, not juxtapose, and the logic not acceptable sim-
ulates the place.
At the point at which the logic is acceptable it disappears,
unknown (it is then that place). So there are two unknowns in
comparison.

The hyena floating to one with the infant in its mouth is
within their convention, is in itself from existence which isn't
produced.
Crowds holding their mouths open, it rains.
The Sudanese fundamentalist government whom 'we're'
supporting is 'allowing' hundreds of thousands of its people to
starve in drought by not allowing relief planes for the famine to
get through, in order to win the war disputing their group's reli-
gious law.

The novel, *The Front Matter, Dead Souls*, was written at the same time as this whole essay, *Objects in the Terrifying Tense*, neck-and-neck, finally exchanging lines throughout crossing over working from one to the other; by having them only existing as separate books, and only repeating in an excerpt, the specific 'place' maintained, it's looking at the events of reality solely.

Lyn Hejinian and I are having a collaboration in which I wrote about having intended to see Venus and a red giant star come close. She was at that moment (when we were to rise) there on the water though not seeing the sky.

From my reply to her:

Just touching but where the one doesn't produce the other.

Not producing, occurring is seeing. It's just appearing on its own. I see my exhaustion at the moment: to be a purely physical contentless condition, which as such is (yet is not from) mental weariness, as the one is of the luminous other, the gold to the fog fishing slowly as an outer occurrence is. The physical exhaustion creates a state which has no mental counterpart even repressed, but that not being a state of resting. The pale sea gold to the fog fishing slowly is a state which has neither counterpart, of one's mental or physical weariness, yet is a luminous outer occurrence then apprehended and is 'apparently' only being awake at dawn (which I wasn't) as nothing.

The artificial, unnatural?, suppression of the physical state makes the luminous event occurring in nature part.

(I have been taking medicine which suppresses my actual physical end/cease of actions:)

The luminous events are so coming into and recognized in

the 'mental state' as its attentiveness, a state which is suppressed; not existing in one's physical state which has been suppressed.

The *physical* life is non-existent, by occurring from suppression, but is occurring by itself.

The various places of attentiveness in this text have 'no' counterpart still by not being repressed. They are not repressed anywhere. It's a wilderness.

If there were rain actually there would be no orb on it either. Then the rim itself's eliminated.

The two lines of comparison aren't separated at all to see what they are.

Our vice president, who links the acceptance of a single mother by the viewers of a T.V. series, which as such is undermining family values to the riots, thinks firing of cities arises from being born.

He should be dumb as cattle.

The image of something real is contemplated as seeing which doesn't exist there. Subject it to seeing which may not ever be its occurrence. Then the image that's real exists solely.

An event is subject to seeing not to its occurrence there. One's seeing it is its sole occurrence.

The handmaiden herself is a tiger who when thrown scraps by the conservative males is enraged in eternity of pain.

They run to them in the little steps, so no one touches existence. They can't be living. When they are. Yelling in the crowd.

For a third, two-thirds, of Thailand, babies, men, and women will die of AIDS. Same in Zaire. India of maybe 800 million living will be the main dying grounds, with no medication. Send me there and seeing any standing still living, not dreaming I will bite them.

They touch me in the bow of dusk.
Torn by jealousy I'll bite infecting them if they're still living.

If any are born ever I'm jealous wanting to live and be there with them.
Bombs drop on lily fields, figures float on them. Fictionalizing is separated so that nothing is omitted.
Nothing drops out from fictionalizing, so it examines itself by including.
Nothing occurring scrutinizes itself. We think that.
Fictionalizing is thinking, conceptualizing is our function.
Pretense is just that fictionalizing too. It doesn't even waver.
This is in comparisons that are dissimilar so as to have them be peaceful when paired.
Where there's no concurrences, the pair's to be peaceful. (Without psyche fragile or separating in rage — which it does — as the basis.)
Surprisingly to myself, the writing won't do that. The form of rage is at times the occurrence; in which spring with blossoming trees say is the occurrence. They're together.
One is in a helpless relation to the rim of nature, which is peaceful.
Newspaper writing has a subject.
It straddles its subject always. It writes on it, in space, it's been eliminated.
A conservative male, who has to have money, has the concept that a subject isn't accurate.
If he's avant garde it's still a subject.

The hyena trotting on the shore slashing at the people as

they wade out from the oil on fire comes from (our) fictionaliz-
ing. It doesn't have to do with conception. They wade up and
are being slashed.

Nature is being socially created yet see it only. It is public
solely.

One can drop the pair, but that's where we live. What's
that?

Raining, the people standing in it still living, one comes up
to them biting to infect them also. Jealous, running at them,
who're in the dusk rim being bitten by me.

My tears are then on a face submerged in the air when I'm
running. That's where I see it here.

The bird falls incinerated in the smoke of black air where
I'm standing in the street and with this narrowing the woman's
rejecting me later, is a comparison on the rim only. It's on the
red ball a retina.

It makes no difference how one responds as long as there is
that.

One leans over looking into the pool of chest gel the man
swimming in it who's serene and gentle. His eyes floating hang-
ing are closed. One needs him for seeing reality. He's hanging in
peace but with one not there.

The man puts his long member in one, bending so he's sit-
ting up on her where the sky's vast and red.

He comes with her in the blue dusk rim which is hanging
under the sky.

There's a vast breath on the sky like a blister.

Yet wounded the soft breath comes from him. The sky's hot,
a blue bowl.

The occurrence in it is in 'ad' time seemingly. One is to be
isolated on the blue dusk rim clear.

It's making a picture of something in order to see it, which is

34

different from simply making a picture. It is between being and becoming so that it is already there.

That's objects as history.

I just realized this writing is passive-aggressive, as a form. If it's on ('seeing') something that's real. It keeps disappearing as the occurrence, as the occurrence does.

So the man lying on the street is in the red line with the bobbing hanging sun. Friendship has to occur there by or from the red line and man.

This is seeing the shape of events of history subject to that arbitrarily seen.

Analyzing the occurrence that can't be seen it splinters in experience infinitely. It recedes continually, causing infinite pain. It isn't even there. People are responsible for the invisible occurrences. That's exciting.

I keep trying to make these pairs of dissimilarity hold to be peaceful, as a form. To have occurrence as them at the same time.

Government prods the people into cattle chutes where they are robbed by bankers and businessmen. It's easiest to rob the public by working right at the bank.

Where there are only actions they neither concur nor float.

Actions make the blue dusk rim.

Kuwaiti royalty, hundreds of whose guest workers as itinerant labor suffered from their imperial yoke and in the aftermath of the war were executed with no trials or fake ones, has to pay to go to bed with Bechtel.

The sumo low scuttles forward on huge crouching legs and pats the other one. There's no content. The open palms slap and slap from the crouching scuttle on the other sumo's chest. One rushes forward with the weight mounted down on the almost kneeling huge legs so that only the palms move in the blows. His haunches scuttle gently.

This is pushed to where being is narrative solely, contentless.

A government can't simply be a business for profit. Then it drops out the people lying on the street who are the inner self.

Schools are not simply businesses but are to cultivate the inner self.

We don't have words at all.

Our vice president tries to turn us against the "cultural elite." Here, the cultural elite are simply people who can read at all.

That's a new poem, as seeing being taken to its first surface.

New

Akira's lying on the black air of dawn. Being in the crowd that is curled on the sidewalk is on the rose line of dawn where there's no perception. Ever.

The chest gel is bared as a glowing worm in the crowd set in the man flat whose limbs are stretched, or rather not themselves but hanging out floating from him in the rose air.

He's just there new, in the black air, so that it's sealed on the rose rim, the only place here.

In the burning lotus fields on water the hyena is coming to them. Swimming, the head just submerged into the black rose rim air. It doesn't swivel but barely moves. The fires around the hyena are ignited but don't give off light, rather the air they are in reflects or creates it.

It's a dense medium. Sunk in this air, they may create it. The heavy pans of the helicopters sinking and rising go by.

The crowd is underneath on a stream. Prostrate floating submerged in the air with the hyena, they have no faculties and that may create it.

The sumo handsome head swaying on the stocks bends. There's a wide bow in the air.

He bends over emerging on the rim.

Lying on the street is at the bottom of dawn, resting there so it's just thinking that.

The rose light so that he's on the rim holding the man, the sumo picks him up in the black air but begins moving bounding like a vast bulb floating on it.

A worm flies to them on the street. The air unfolds in the silk suit softly billowing to them faintly in it. As it meets them, the man held by the sumo swims out slashing it. His projecting from the arms of the sumo, they're buoyed so not from each other.

The green hump lies peacefully no eyes floating on the sky.

Eyes closed floating, gazing downward inside, on the rim of dawn he's slashing swaying out at the worm flying to them then.

To the sumo, as it flies to them, sealed in the air, this appears in the purple as skewered ruffled billows, flattened and dead so as to only be in the widened air.

That's floating in it where the rim is lost too.

I can't find the relation to this.

But one would have to loosen it utterly to pick up on the dusk air that's on dawn.

One's not in that, so can't exert force to find it. Or floating on it is on the occurrence, where there's no forcing going on.

Seeing what we all see is floating on the occurrence.

Where only some diverging from it, emerges on our actual air. Actions only are the occurrence. Any could be not dreamed.

The point of reading is just to read, per *se*, so that real actions are submerged in our air. They're on the blue, bulbous air, inflated.

The wildly coagulating heavy sides of the helicopter go over again so that those underneath crouch in the pea air where the sumo carrying Akira in it flaps.

A larger range has been opened on a horizontal frame where the sumo flaps in the dense coagulation but so thick they're not moving in the beam which only reflects the pea stream.

There's no eye floating. That's in Akira hanging down now, the sockets hanging are carried. His comforting presence is still calming as long as he's living.

No one's a function for being calm yet without him the dis-similarities on the pea stream are held and aren't peaceful (when living). That's interesting. The pea stream narrows a track to 'natural' death, what else is there, while before it is society, yet having any concept is inaccurate where something occurs. On it.

So there's only the occurrence on the stream with him

or being utterly lost, as if there were souls . . . .

Robert Grenier's 'Scrawl'

Robert Grenier's 'scrawl' is comparable to Stan Brakhage's films which Brakhage described as poems.

Grenier's 'book' is drawing, which has no other translation ('reading') than its pictorial being ('shape'). Using Stan Brakhage as a foil, in the film Reflections on Black the filmmaker has scratched with a sharp instrument over a blind man's eyes so that a set of brilliant white stars shimmers on the film stock itself. Attacking the surface of the film and reflecting on the conditions of film-making is making consciousness.

Grenier's poems are drawings which are 'drawn' as if from the other side of the paper. As if he writes with his left hand.

(He actually did write some of the pages that way.) His text is scratchings on an original space existing only in that; and as if it were on the other side of the paper at the same time. Another sense of space is created.

In the book's first section, the composition of the 8-1/2 x 11 pages is an act of politics. You've *got* to get everything onto the page, and it *can* only be 18 pages. (This section was originally published as an ABACUS (Potes & Poets Press) issue, the format of which is 18 pages on 8-1/2 x 11).

The final episode is introduced by scratches of stars bursting on black leader, as if we too were seeing through the blind man's eyes.

The reader of these poems has to decipher (as really seeing) them. Pages are sometimes divided by a line (center line of notebook), that have a reflecting upside-down 'image' on the bottom; that are the graphic rendition of poems which echo and in some way also 'empty out' the 'other' image. Or are just the next poem in the notebook.

They just exist in that space, which is also 'non-translatable' (in the sense of an act of politics) as not graphic or 'fine art' in its material or technique. In a sense, it can't be translated (it's opaque) because it's xerox: both individuated and continually different *and* mass produced. It is as if the correspondences and reflections are produced from the text being a mass technique.

Grenier's experimentation with xerox as graphic art is form which enables drama and 'characters' to be seen in a new way. Brakhage's infants being born, or scenes of children playing with themselves are such an abstract form or 'scrawl'.

Grenier's text is a form of love poem comprised of three parts. In the first part, "What I Believe," the poet addresses Kathleen Frumkin; in the second part "Transpiration/ Transpiring," he makes "a little magic book" to endeavor to imagine "what else is in the world," and is cast on transformation/itself/ "only hope" in which this literal shape is the form of the world (such as in the drawing of the moon as a skull with the writing scrawled in that space "I'll try to draw / the Moon last / night — it was / like this").

The finding of the world is the writing of shapes, moving to the (horizon) recognition that there is "no end to shapes" or translations in the word/world.

The third section, "Minnesota," constitutes a movement of integration in sound and shape, rising to a love poem to a loon (moon) and the loon's love song to the moon. The latter occur on split double-reflecting pages in a simplicity of beauty arrived at only by the prior process of the (going there) decipherment of the handwriting.

These poems are an attempt to have the 'word' ('world') read as 'world' ('word') as a form of "societal function" or love. It is created by an author being made imaginary to, thus in a sense created by, a reader who translates.

Robert Grenier's 'poems', in another series, *rhymms*, from notebooks produced using color xerox, are drawn superimposed on each other in different colors so that their meaning and reading are the same in that imposition.

The words of his text are simply nature as angelic.

The phrases' meaning/reading isn't other than their entwined imposition in being drawn.

He is subjecting thought/words to analysis by their being their drawn shape.

As if 'our'-(real society's)-opposed-to analysis is the corollary of such a superimposition.

Their own shape analyzes them. And the shape he draws does not distort them.

My observation is that a social extension of 'our' view (of analysis) occurs as a corollary becoming apparent (as if reflected in the drawn impositions he makes).

The writing can only be read as the dual enmeshed, sometimes four color, images are *seen*.

This is not determined by or accessible to memory.

In the color xerox writing, the figures/letters are interspersed on the page, one color being read, a layer only distinguishable from words in another color; so color is an indication of time but in which the words/layer in one color are neither 'before' or 'after' those in another color.

The green drawn "I am a beast" is identical with (is written

41

on) the blue "my heart is beating" enmeshed in that space. They are enmeshed isolated as their entity as color, not subject to language even.

To open 'content'/behavior/thought to its drawn shape changes the nature of that content so that it's seen as image/word only — or it's seen only.

Its meaning is the function of its occurrence.

Reasoning is not present in the enmeshed images' space? The enmeshed image in the space has relation to our reasoning. Yet words such as 'spirit' are not simply their drawn image. Grenier doesn't subject 'spirit' to being only in that space, as drawn.

Reasoning's not present any more than spirit, if one is to see the enmeshed line/word only (simply).

Reasoning is subject to the space created in which the enmeshed images 'arise', by its not being present — or (not being) eliminated.

Why isn't the same rigor exerted on the word 'spirit'; in not doing so it is as if there were image outside of its occurrence?

Grenier's space is only occurrence (what is real); so 'spirit' (the word is an assertion which describes a 'given' socially understood, allows us to be in that given frame) should be eliminated except as it is occurring as a fact/shape on the page?

('Spirit' can't be identified as a traditional word or form, as it only *occurs* as the real, which is in the present.)

Grenier's words are sometimes drawn on no horizon.

A line is subjected to that space.

(I'm trying to 'see' his rigor in my sentences. The intention is to be within the way his text sees, and to place a comparison beside that seeing — which allows *both*.)

In his text, the image/word has no meaning except as occurrence which is seen only where there's no horizon, except the lines dividing the page.

Rather, Grenier's superimpositions are the actual horizon

line on the edge/meaning of the poetic line.

His thought has a shape that isn't 'nature' either or is it as well.

What I Believe Transpiration / Transpiring Minnesota,
Robert Grenier, O Books, Oakland, 1992

Dual Memory

The Scarlet Cabinet is a dual collection of the works of Alice Notley and Douglas Oliver, as such a most interesting idea as union of two minds.

Considering Notley's poem "Beginning with a Stain:"

The writing, and probably also what Notley calls the "heart," is a series of continual starting points in which what was there wasn't prior; but always was there because at the same time it's the only existing point(s).

Somehow everything exists walking on water by being projected in a sense of time. It materializes.

> There was already somebody there, at the
> beginning of creation, there's a great calm though
> with water to walk upon
> . . . I'm going to love you, I
> already do because I'm already
> walking on the still, Oceanic Earth (p. 352)

Similarly, the action of the heart which couldn't be prior to its object, is. "Born in beauty, born a loved one, before history." It knows without learning. It is the writing, prior to being formed.

There are links between actions known without contemplating. "I will never not make a sound, not have made a sound / I will ride this voice as I change, as always am."

This occurs between peoples. Memory is an action. 'The Cheyenne who are suffering' occurs as a memory in the writing.

This constitutes knowing what one could not in life have known (since it is prior); and it's known objectively in the writing.

The action of the heart is as much time-fixed as the continual action of death; we only love in relation to starting points. Recognizing this continual openness is disrupting, as the recognition of it is itself the most precarious point.

Openness is more precarious even than the deaths (of those loved) which are the foci of this poem, "the part of the mind that wears no mask; and you."

Thus holding onto grief continually creates the observation, that is itself being the action of openness.

That openness is the tongued heart speaking. That's all there is (for everyone).

> first heart of. O human, your heart must be that
>   heart
> Sail out this morning & look at your city
> I am afraid

This is a hard criterion for existence.

You're known as an entity, which is probably your multitudinous actions: "they know who you are in eternity / (one of the hells)."

One is emptied out by a relation to the Cheyenne, and to others ("I dreamed it to the bottom of myself").

Already coded and has happened, one lives backward through history and becomes original beginnings.

Writing now is the means of entering existence, as directions, as was *The Egyptian Book of the Dead*.

The Language of Heaven:
The dead in the shape of the writing, the sound not spoken, are the same as the living, there. It's known only there as the poem's 'measure', is it. That (living and dead being the same) is a relation in reality.

45

The correspondence of the dead and the living, their identity/sameness, is in the sound (shape) of the poem; remains in it not as spoken.

Notley sees this 'identity' and 'measure' without social construction, in the poem.

The conception of feeling (in real society), which makes intellect distinct from one's natural mind which is intellect, is itself "human-made humanness."

Notley uses "feeling" as being clarity. The condensed measure takes place as a reasoning, is the form, and is based on "exhaustion of reasoning."

A space is created that is neither the reasoning nor our construction of the "bagged body" that is "human-made humanness." ("you've bagged you all up, all around . . . If the bag breaks, the real you, comes out.")

This shape that's apprehended is neither sound nor picture except as a space where the dead and living are the same, "a flat blue, that's the sky . . . that blue's the blue bagged body." Apprehension is 'as if drawn' (picture). Similar to H.D., the reasoning 'sees' the relationships/the space only, with no transformative capacity for analysis, except as it's vision that is outside of the horizon line in the flat blue sky, is culture too.

The writing can only see the real, the ordinary. Notley subjects the relation of the real dead and living to the shape interiorly as writing; similar to Robert Grenier's superimposed phrases that are read only as that dual shape not to be memory or reasoning.

'Human-made humanness' is subject to the shape (that's interior to writing). 'Human-made humanness' cannot be with the delicate shape.

The shape of the writing (which is feeling and the relation of the dead and living) is created by the shape interiorly, as if not as it's socially constructed. That shape of writing is not subject to one's reasoning, though it's a form of one's reasoning, removed.

There, a shape that can't be seen 'in life' occurs not being solely within its language shape.

Feeling isn't running against anything (in a way).

Intellect is running against itself meeting itself to see the flat blue sky.

The Scarlet Cabinet, Douglas Oliver & Alice Notley, Scarlet Editions, New York, 1993.

Objects in the Terrifying Tense
Longing from Taking Place

What's Modern

What's modern is always an embryo encased in nourishment and held together by a fragile but durable thread of something or other. — Carla Harryman

Carla Harryman creates paragraphs (in *The Words*) designating hierarchy of objects in which the basis of hierarchy and comparison itself is extended to emptiness. Parroting the nihilist's formula which posits nothing 'behind' comparison, there is only the formula itself. This is regarded as Authority *per se*.

By parroting this function 'back' there is no plot.

Short phrases separated by commas (phrases of equal worth) in extended sentences form these paragraphs which are internal songs.

The light expanding paragraph is "a portable icon left over from the burning pages of an appropriated culture's bell-tome."

The language of artificial jungles that is appropriated culture is both incomprehensible to "our unproven universe" ('our' inner comparison) and a parroting of it.

Therefore "We" who are viewers, personages, flattened seen as juice egg beetles, golden, permanent children are held in a backwash that is also moving forward in the agar (something lighter than that, floating) of the long paragraph. What's modern is as conditional as any of the other details created by the "bogus specialist." This dismisses his story.

The writing is entirely 'created by' statements which are series of 'bogus' constructs as if the offshoot of the bogus specialist. Statements prompted our quest for shadow games. Functions and the shadow games themselves are similar statements.

The narrator is an undesignated "we"/"our" applying 'its' "pragmatic response" to actors named like icons or allegory by their functions, such as "All Done," "All-the-Loss-That-Ever-Was," the "Romanticized-Hell-Grabbers" or the family "The Dailys." As desires are not designated they're vast.

Via these thin surfaces, what's occurring goes on in the paragraph different even from the realm of our desires: "Since from the outside we were viewed as innocuous, placid, or coincidental, our inner surges were protected from interference. In fact this view, so divergently propped above our own appetites, permitted us tremendous territory over the realm of our own desires, desires that were never named and that remain inchoate to this day."

There is the illusion of spontaneous creation without our noticing it.

The sense of Harryman's "we" is of a familiar context separated from others. Or is it We? If we are creating the illusion and what we are creating goes unnoticed continually, there is no space in between in the context (in the long paragraph) in which creation is hanging.

The beginning and the end (of narrative) are together, unknown: "There amidst debris, or a punctuating smile, or any such things that by their purely independent objecthood induce an illusion of spontaneous creation while all the while hidden away their producers recreate them everyday, we entertained small animals and no one noticed."

Immediately following the paragraph which ends with the

above, there is no space; space is collapsed in the sense that "The answer to one question is obvious, and the answer to the other is there is only one subject." If there is only one subject, the paragraph is a black hole. All creation occurs outside of this space, while the context of this hypothetical space is asserted. All Done holds forth on the historical loop of desire.

A blank space, filled with sensation, occurs. "Inquiry leaves us on the stage, physically overdeveloped and exposed."

It is this unmapped terrain of sensation which is not designated or known as such which occurs in Harryman without us knowing where or when.

It may be arrived at 'negately', as otherwise it would be known. There is no place for it. "It tells about the ugly wart-like sandwich child located in a doctor's distant jargon. It is not sexy. It is not vicious. It is not the underworld, though the crackpot in a drugstore reads stanzas staples to a hush. The crackpot's echo hurts the child whose fine-tuned bell has limits."

There's no nihilist or All Done as theory, no primordial swamp of psyche/eroticized-underworld, which is itself theorized; and it exists as an 'echo' hurting the child which is a clear empty bell.

Is the permanent child one or one displaced and never allowed through it?

The child is originally empty as a bell not in the romanticized sense; in the sense actually occurring in the long paragraph which empties. The beginning is emptied by the end, the end which in the uniform extension is seen to be empty.

The Words is not a novel because it is 'uniform throughout'. The characters who are objects, we flattened children, or figures who are permitted to be images so long as they are functions disappear or appear without connection to plot, only creating space in that area where there is none.

Where there aren't magic fatal worldly eyes, romanticized

expressions: "what makes them an image and not a living object."

Harryman is undercutting the image which is not a living object by 'undercutting' the living object. In this negative space on negative space, the child we floats on a spool.

The comparison of the image and the living object, as if there is nothing else, is that space where the burning child is father to the woman or the hard child is mother to the man.

The magic fatal worldly eyes that are no longer existing as the narrator perceive the spool with the child on it.

Thus the narration is not passive in that there are not images that are valid to the objectified surface (as the objectified/theorized surface is bogus). Also, some dissonant, not-romantic 'beauty' occurs that is neither the inchoate or the theorized surface. It is 'beauty' in the sense of phenomena, not conclusive.

Merely Modern

The form of the rondeaux creates a text which is remembering back, to the present.

One can see comparisons between the phenomena of the texts (which are mentioned in this essay). The comparisons one makes are a memory of the present.

This description is to be history by being only in present time without events, not representation. The view of the present is together, as a Bosch landscape of Heaven, Hell, and Earth is (this changes continually by being seen as if from the perspective of those who are in it). There is a narrative in the fact of their proximity yet not figurative, not existing in being representation. 'Doing others' movements' as writing, are details in it or my 'reproductions' (as if after it) by being present time only.

The rondeaux is in the present, with no beginning or end,

by its repetitions maintaining a middle. It can only be so by that which is occasional occurring throughout.

In Laura Moriarty's *Rondeaux*, the occasional (the sense of haphazard, open admission of anything, "Each page says anything") occurs at the beginning and ending line, emphasizing or maintaining the middle time.

The portions of Moriarty's book which use the playful, circular form of the rondeaux creating the middle are then mirrored in the book that doesn't have a map, that is 'without' that form, as if to "refer to time as eternity."

The timing of the writing makes statements about its own structure because it disallows its/one's representation by history. By being its own subject it mocks and reforms representation itself. "Cool under the structures provided by subjects," which are both 'topics' and oneself as a subject and 'subjected', is now representation itself.

One is inside 'representing' it (the process of representing and of making history). Mimicking the circular day-to-day she mimics 'history category' by resembling its rim.

Its minute motions are timing. Yet this is only the appearance. *It* doesn't exist.

Nor does the 'subject'.

This is because the middle is one's 'speaking directly' in present time/is actual. There is no life that is description; similar to Creeley, the 'speaker' is only timing, divided/split (as the form she's using) as one's beginning and end: "As if divided I write you and see / Each page handing it over directly / You at the same time / in a speech / Make writing into life."

Speech is 'lecture'. We're 'spoken to' by category/real rim history. It is also 'speaking directly' which can occur only if the 'you' exists receiving it at the same time. She reinstates 'the other' by the rondeaux being timing, keeping track and speaking at the same time "From the middle of my life to the middle of yours."

It is an old form which is not speech itself, or hearing, but rather absence of such. There is the "equivalent" of breath or sighs. These are merely represented in the text and are not heard while hearing 'you'.

Any speaker is necessarily divided by reality: "Why am I divided thoughtlessly?" Hearing, speaking, and timing are reducing time to a negative space, which is in the 'fixed form': "All things reduced to the absence of these / Same things They rush me to return / On time or even before I've gone and said."

The rondeaux being the repetitive daily round that's real, one is not the same as it nor does one diverge from being in it. One is in the middle, of or 'between', not in, those conditions.

The relation of speaking to timing is to make the same as content which is thus that negative space. There being no subject, while subjected absently, it is freed at the same time as being realistic: "And to brave clearness or to what we have instead."

Moriarty's use of system is similar to the monk in Pasolini's film *The Hawks and the Sparrows* having been told to convert the birds, praying on his knees before them for days. They rush at him converted finally. Asked by a younger monk, how he did it, he answers I'm not a saint so I had to use my brains.

The characteristic of the 'fixed form' is that it "thinks only of itself." The self is emptied out by the form's beginnings and endings.

We long for reality because it takes place. The negative space is 'creating' a place where the self isn't, and where the 'other' isn't; by being reduced to the absence of these, the text is erotic not simply by withholding but as the reverse statement to touch the rim of occurring.

That is utterly confident not from oneself but from what's accurate. This is *stated* inaccurately as it's occurring.

The male is restated by the text making *his* statement overt ly: "She occupies a place occupied by Goddesses and Queens because she is an open secret. The King is here because he came back. What became reinstated was his ability to negotiate with his minions. They have no dimensionality either. The fountain appeared in the middle as an image of plenty."

Him reinstating his relations to his minions, where she is an open secret, is not her relation to him. It's his relation to her. There's a separation in what's perceived in communication that is the erotic text itself.

Communication itself destabilizes, by either disrupting or imitating the 'fixed form' (of structure, poetic and social) which thus is negative space by being an 'open' secret. Both 'reverse languages' existing in the same space cancel each other out: "He has taught me his language And I him mine These verses equally unstable Recognize themselves In the broken running taught to soldiers."

Precisely by playing in that circle which is statement of the King's language by everyone, it is reversed in space, she is the King's whore, he opened her mouth "When everyone gets to be King and speak this beautiful language."

As in Creeley's form, one is repressive.

If everyone's king in speaking the same, which is 'regarded' as the only reality, reverse statements are the unknown being spoken. The 'fixed form' relocates as parts: "Heads filled the picture. I couldn't recognize myself. I could have been anybody." She cancels negation by evening it, expanding it.

Negative space is where there is no assignment. That itself is produced by the military. Absence is actually reproduction negatively. The event occurs backward. This occurs by repeating the militaristic catechism. Crowds are seen separate from it therefore.

The military produces the reverse of 'one's' life. Both are repressive as emanating from 'one.'

54

Life, the event, and separation are occurring at the same time. "The crowd opens up before her simultaneously mute"; which is 'speaking itself'.

All occurs on the same level at once.

Statement is modern because it is *not* present time. It can't ever *be*. The text 'refers' to the modern which is therefore separation. There being only a one statement, it is: "merely modern, impossible to maintain because made of questionable materials."

That which states itself (as modern) which is militaristic catechism, is "The background collage." So there is no time, as we are free of this catechism. If it's expanded, we can't be in it.

Moriarty's text is therefore statement to be that collage as timing. The 'original' collage is "unquestionable as it was intermittent" (because it *is* so at present). By 'maintaining' those intermittent absences, a structure of absences, the reverse statement which occurs of soft porn is the negative and really open, playful space: "The impossibility finally of owning anything began to oppress him."

Reverse of statement, as a round, is *continually* present time. Moriarty's use of 'fixed form' is at times a soft porn that's reversed as being intimacy really, never fixing, a sense of security and completion emanating from it.

Represented Objects

But still life is poor evidence of what those represented objects are when they are not under observation. — Erica Hunt

The comparison of the image to the living object is occurrence as rim of observation, in the comparison of these texts. One is seeing their observation of the object, as an image, to see.

Erica Hunt's use of the past tense in *Local History* is so that description represents objects/oneself as lifeless, rather than being what they are (when not under observation). To remove observation of the object is *not* to represent it.

As a corollary, structure in the writing is to be only a simple projection of even minute experience. The past tense finds origin as structure diverging from experience: "so divergent was the commotion of the city's frame from the means to operate it."

(In scientific observation, what's alive now is old and becoming more simple; 'ancient' life, before dinosaurs, was young and structurally more complex and varied.)

We repeat the replicant structure of experience and of mythologies without knowing meaning, 'their's' or 'one's.'

Her writing is utterly simple, description itself, and visible: "The idea we harbor is subversive . . . A complete thought in the center of our most visible selves."

This is to be the writing's own converse. We can't see objects/(oneself) without transforming them so one has to forget them as their description.

History is merely continuous, repeating the new: "History acquires its perfect specificity in succeeding versions."

The real city swallows the evidence of one's arrival, the past; the replica of the city proliferates forgeries so one doesn't know one's origin.

The poetic text is utterly simple to not be history. (This essay can't be either.) Where there is no history, and is only simplicity, one observes one's origin of self.

So velocity enables us to see the real and the replica together (as the same?): "One travels at a velocity necessary to see both cities . . . in hieroglyphs."

One can't ever enter the location where one is to be with oneself, except by remembering small events, individualized.

The writing cannot break into the feedback simulation of

56

reality except as remembering the minute motions of oneself/others, because violence which *is* that simulated reality *per se* would only be duplicated by its entry or existence in the writing. So the ordinary small life, and description of it being such, in the writing is *not* a replica of violence or simulation itself:

by being so, the description of simulation, seen to be doing that gently.

Actions, which are not interpreted, are reunited with one, having a deathless life outside of the life apparently producing them. Repression causes memory: "When the memory reappears, having unaccountably lived a deathless and reckless life on its own, it inundates my forecast of grimy blankness, opens the door to where I live now."

Neither the substance nor the organization of her writing is transparent; nor is either constructed (determined) by juxtaposition: "In the free press everything would have to be aggressively connected or related or mismatched, to make organization transparent where substance is not."

In this writing, organization does not determine even her 'utopia'. After the image on the retina, there's no violence as rendering of it, nor is there ordering of it. Such an order would be simulation itself.

Light itself being composed by experience is the observer. The writing is not to represent experience but (after) to be utterly simple composed by it.

Translation of the Grid

Composed of 270 14-line stanzas using the model of Pushkin's *Evgeny Onegin*, *Oxota: A Short Russian Novel*, is a form of chronicle which is continuous and nonlinear and puts detail of Lyn Hejinian's life abroad in Russia as if a grid to experience itself, puts the writing to present change itself.

The writing is a mediation or translation of the inner warp of two cultures, her own and Russian, in a time in history in which enormous force is passing through the Russian context in which she observes. Hejinian wants to come to the point of realizing everything has changed, and as one can't know the exact moment or instance of transition, to create a form of swimming screen or grid: "I have not isolated the active element of my medium — my / medium is mediation / Aesthetic impression swimming clockwise . . . / An enormous force passes through — we want urgently to / know what changes."

Oxota's (the word means "the hunt") screen is a form of inherent conflict and of "The excitation of the same experience by two grammars."

It's in the center as comparison of 'life'.

Sleep is a grid put to instability of volition, to willfulness and intention. Everyday life is a grid put to sex. The writing is "inexhaustible faculty of negation — it puts grammar to the hunt" as the process of translation; and is also a grid of, in that sense opposed to, experience.

"Yet both awake and asleep the process of translating matter into memory continued."

It is as if experience must be eliminated, or be passive, in order for the self to be. There is "A loss of self with a high level of content." Experiences are not the self. The mind is active; it's as if experiences are ghosts which arise before the occurrence of life (p. 43), that is, before the mind's translation into and as its own realm.

Experience has to be subsumed to be exactly in the center. The mind and occurrence in life come together from separate directions.

It is experience itself which conceptually is falsification of oneself, not just conventional narration of experiences. This conception in *Oxota's* form is the faculty of negation stripping Hejinian's own experiences so as to not determine their outcome or history.

The conception that form is rigorous analysis ("Form subjugates every experience") is based on the chosen form being continuous and including aberrations, change, and disruption ("The absurd occurrence could come between sun").

After its observation of itself, "Total disappearance is the goal of each activity."

Reality is neutral and so experience must be neutral to see either.

Hejinian's intention is "optical clarity at all levels." Sexuality does not need to contend. She hypothesizes a "normal" mind, a harmonious source as the basis of accurate observation in the process of writing which is continuous and inclusive, as if to propose otherwise were romantic or posturing: "Is real life prophetic if its details are typical / The unconstructed life cannot have been invented."

This is putting rational schemata to violent historical change. The separation of event from self leaves events without origin or relation to each other.

Where they appear to coalesce the self is imposed to separate, by being our cultural relativity, rational schemata. (The self is thus made a given that appears 'neutral'.) It produces details, the same as produced by 'reality itself.'

So as not to invent its schemata, mode of perception of it.

Not to have an image of it (*its* 'lens' or schemata), is to have writing only. This is apparently to rid writing of that image, of itself.

As such, the self is apparently not only not determined by history, but history occurs without it; so the self is isolated as one put to 'history' as received structure which doesn't exist. 'History' is empty by emptying 'experience': "However there is a danger that life, being narrated, will turn into an 'adventure', and every adventure moves inexorably towards resolution — but how can I say that I don't like adventure? / I think now of the truly startling antiquity of the sensation that *this is happening*."

An adventure is the individual in 'neutral' reality. (This is *my* construct. Perhaps Hejinian has the construct of a 'neutral self' *and* a 'neutral reality' in which what is seen occurs by their extension and confluence.)

Hejinian may regard adventure as constructing a life, as if accounting of event is determinism *per se*, resolution as per narrative form. It seems to *me* that a 'series of adventures' is history without a deterministic frame (of interpretation) imposed, and subject to a high level of disruption. Implicit in *Oxota* is the lack of connection of the individual to experience so that 'experience' itself is subliminal. Male and female are together. Writing crosses the grid to it.

Uniting is happening secretly which is culturally as the forbidden 'inner' self. This concept of forbidden self is 'us'; as it is seen from our culture, it's 'relativistic'.

Hejinian's 'subject' is a high resistance to crossing by which this itself sometimes achieves a subliminal level of "Sleeping past the depression that reality divides." One such subliminal touching of the grid to experience is the story of the ram who having a job leading the other rams and sheep to slaughter ("Sleeping between itself and not itself . . . . the corpses behind and the ram ahead") one day refuses to do so and is itself slaughtered. It is simply replaced.

Translating two separate strands, two cultures, to each other oneself disappears. Just not doing rational schemata or doing it continuously causes the subliminal also.

The slaughter of the leading ram, as if repression, is juxtaposed against the image of Bambi as "normal": "A face so familiar and one sees that it expresses something in / life that we have seen on that face / Alone, after work, things were happening to it."

The notion that form subjugates every experience is opened there to the thought that reality is such a form; and events in it are not continuous or comprehensible. There is no system to reveal: "I can't escape reality . . . . events are conspicuous but not continuous."

To invent is groundless, inner. She extends generously.

'The continuous (life) writing is not invented' implies a basis of comparison, used as a form.

Not to 'invent' is reality. The place of comparison (maximum stress) may be either (or both) being at the point where experience and mind are divided, or at the point where they have imploded on each other.

A line may carry over the margin edge to be continued as paragraph as an infinite inclusive line. The 14-line stanza 'fixed form' is passed. The line's 'eliminated' to infinity.

Hejinian puts cultural division and difference as a grid to 'non-event'. 'Modernism recognized things, postmodernism disperses them'.

Postmodernist displacement puts things in places, she says, and what is experienced is the intensity of empty places.

Language is a grid on time and the conception of self is the event.

The Cell is a long series of days, dated, as if the account/assembly of 'events' infinite on those days and placing (comparing) the self to 'the event horizon' can see where memory, a fiction itself, isolates in real infinity by resembling it: "Out of it things fell / very close — no time / Throughout space confusion — memory, that / separation from infinity."

The Event Horizon

Agnes Martin with her infinity of 'uniform' brush marks that are devoid of event in utter concentration is similar in minimalist painting to Mei-mei Berssenbrugge's relation to language. Both are engaged in a meditation on nature seen in its phenomenal emptiness, analyzed from the perspective of itself: "space turns into a projection of itself, like dreaming about dreams."

Empathy is a graph that is purely relational. The process of abstraction, and analysis from that, makes the phenomenal moment inclusive, transparent: "and then making transparent with abstractions, such as in the phenomenal moment or with coincidence, / because everything can be told from the present moment. Its sort of transparent experience / begins to develop in which things are really precise without depending on each other. / In this way she takes the principles of abstraction, founded on sight, and applies them to language. / When she does this, a non-visual abstraction occurs, sometimes with the naturalistic edge."

Events do not depend on each other yet act on each other and are apprehended, changing, in a non-visual form while arising from visual and sensory observation.

One can perceive events as a contemplation of nature without the meaning given to them in social ordering, while at the same time allowing that ordering as a factor of nature.

The 'ordering' of the apprehension in the writing is not imposed from one's psyche only, however much effort took place to contemplate this reality.

Psyche is another factor of nature which while ordering it cannot be apprehended visually.

So Berssenbrugge's writing doesn't posit a negative space, or rather does in the long lines on which minute relations have equality creating an implicit stretch of infinity which analyzes by being inclusive. The writing is a "relational state" in which non-human perspective is as much a factor as human perspective; nor is this anthropomorphic, rather the opposite, an infinite extension of perspective and possible relations of perspectives: "as the horizon when you are moving can oppose the horizon inside."

How does she do this calmly as the means of the relational state?

Sight is as much an event (which qualitatively changes the event seen) as is 'original' event. This concentration and reciprocal changes arising from it is "the event horizon": "When her attention is discontinuous, this no longer means that she / is inattentive."

To be 'inattentive' merely widens the perspective. The horizon cannot keep out.

This purely relational graphing in which the experience itself is the continual restatement of its structures ("that is being born, and as it becomes, its being is received structure"), is the "subject's removal from the work" by its/Berssenbrugge's continual removal (as delineated as a modern condition by Barrett Watten in *Conduit* : "it indicates only the limits of the writer's form, as incoherent and various as that might be. It is not by any means what he is 'saying'. Nothing can be compelled from the site of the speaker except the outlines of his form.")

To narrow to the outlines of its form (*as per* Watten) is utter scrutiny, is real.

It's the interior relation of experience.

Not collapsing in absence, the limits of her form are calmly placed against the limits of his form, outside of the mass that is an experience, the site of each changing.

Berssenbrugge posits the reconstituting of location (and/by observation of it), in which the human is only a part of the whole structure so that observation is occurring from phenomena and from the structure itself (so that we can see that).

The perspectives of received structure are only illuminating however destructive: "a category of gray dots / on a television screen of star data, representing no one's experience, / but which thrills all who gaze on it, so it must be experience."

Berssenbrugge uses a lens to examine a lens. The conception of seeing itself is art, cultural phenomena rather than 'direct experience'. Yet culture is being experience, that is not visual. The picture of simultaneous absence and presence arises from the space of not being there: "there's no way he or she can jump from anything continuous, such as a line, to anything discrete, / such as points, both continuous and discontinuous are real, or models / as near to reality as we get, due to a kind of fundamental ignoring oneself. / Yet, even the model has progressed beyond simultaneous continuity and discontinuity / to a picture of simultaneous presence and absence."

The writing is in the separation, the ignoring oneself, which produces the simultaneity.

Disruption is not a basis for this.

Absence has a relation to the unfinished.

Erotic is not determined by or a condition of disruption. "She" and "Your" are not separated.

Change can sweep across the whole structure, is even retroactive.

In *Sphericity*, when a point is silent, it's not a vantage point. Really there's no vantage point, and the instant of apprehension *is* solely. The event horizon is so loaded, the horizon's everywhere: " — the seam, my experience of your experience, a horizon at dawn, is the instant of apprehension."

———

Our disruption of the 'given' relations to each other is our 'subjective' 'ego' 'groundless' 'fragmentation' which analyzes.

The corollary of this is that disruption of the 'given' is analysis only when there is not belief in (its) analysis.

Irreconcilable relations are flattened to be one while maintaining their conflict, contained in a person. It was more difficult to hold them apart.

Cultural duality is on the poetic line (the line of writing), throughout. One has to be in inner conflict for that reconciliation.

One could within the writing achieve reconciliation calmly, like Berssenbrugge or Hejinian. Both indicate that a mode is not to be valued in itself.

What's present is the comparison, the putting of thought which is light, fragile, to life/dying/war: relations it can't sustain such as bathos qualifies light thought. Scrutiny qualifies the structure, is it. The structure is now expansive and light also.

Experience itself is subliminal now.

The line widens or disappears to have multiple strains in it.

While 'being extreme is subjective' that is being groundless now. Where the basis is 'masculine' 'tradition', 'subjective' is groundless; we have to be groundless.

To take that into consideration, to what it is compared to, is realistic.

The comparison of relations in a form (which is 'the control group', merely the basis of comparison) makes transparent both the "Romanticized-Hell-Grabbers" and the "bogus specialist." 'Groundless' is then the basis of comparison.

Sundown is a red line — they (the ball on the red line) have no relation to existence, or nature there.

The horizon can't keep out in being on itself, in nature.

Comparison of relations discs imposed on each other analyzes all grounds of comparison.

If we ourselves are objects in the terrifying tense, our writing reflects the object of oneself. It reflects back the object seen through 'their' eyes to 'them'.

The line (writing) is the preconscious of others. The preconscious imposed on their eyes is also where it's known then.

Does erotic produce the preconscious object?

"Objects in the Terrifying Tense
Longing from Taking Place"

Now not as 'doctrine', one can't cleave to or be 'masculine' 'tradition' which is non-existent as we're together floating with real individuals. This is the only love. There is no separation between essay and poetry.

On the other side of this *one* standard corresponds "the stone soldier," the end of history being happy if the child is of the happy mean, the mean being the center of the dual columns where one is able to see from there being no symmetry (ever) which occurs as "crowded by symmetry."

All actions are equalized on the "crowded symmetry" mocked and mocking, straddling, a 'history' already happy, known, so that one/all are totally isolated and alone as one is resembled — "I am asleep I am dead I am found."

Observation of the present can't occur otherwise. The present appears continually. It is a preconscious object which linear 'tradition' is also.

One has no existence in the language continually in order to found "a smaller ground base" of not existing in the mean.

The general ("returns things through things") translates backwards or inversely to the small ground so that actions (which are in the middle, the mean) 'history', the fake origin, is straddled not having produced oneself.

The 'general' 'origin' cannot produce the present. So the one ("the singer reads absence backwards") can arise from her own lyricism, which is relativistic within its own fictional terms.

The beginning of Norma Cole's *Metamorphopsia* is pages

with dual columns discrete yet 'comparing' their relation, that of the two columns. They do not run over, so the "Insoluble letters" of the text, mysterious, beautiful like Breughels, are seen only by the fact of their brief congruence here and there in oneself/the reader as forming a relation to oneself in its "given distance / insoluble."

The relational standard being to oneself which is composed of borrowed fragments or echoes of some order, the text is a fragile scrutiny: "congruence / always very brief / some ocean of / obstacle actual (in / yourself) one stan- / dard or the other / *borrowed* at the / core of who looks / for what's lost *as* / *if* pass away for- / mally near to makes / two of you."

Only "particle statement" made as a reflection of the imposed symmetry (everything is false history) by being reflected makes the dual base for real "actions region."

The "Government of a thing," whether the institution of governments or our ordering of reality, is completely empty so the double columns reflect a concealed, known repression of eroticism as well as a "restful figure / without history."

The subject is gone — which is 'its', 'oneself', 'frame'. The fake origin and oneself reading it are both "preconscious by its absence."

The "false topography reflecting different intentions and starving" does not make her lyricism by estrangement, because "there is no sensory deception in fiction."

One sees that 'it' is repressed in oneself so that one sees the connection between non-events and non-events:

> a secret hill always dear
> separated from the last horizon
> endless setting and watching
> silence in fingers separated a little
> wind, seasonal vocal comparison
> comes in, pulls a person's hair out
> ducks a person in the sea

There not being any paradise either in history or 'oneself' (paradise has no events), the fake origin is restored to its "original strangeness." The trait of discontinuity (and no origin) is its reality: "unable to isolate matter from its phenomena / discontinuity jumps even out of time."

The false topography itself enables one to "diagram cities beyond dimensions 'in lovely blue'" where "comparisons move as sails."

Backwards lyricism that is "cracked by symmetry," rather than being 'the' imposed symmetry, crosses the columns.

It reveals a dimensionless "gelatin filled up with behavior / starving discolored things / that is, faces made not to last / of course in time suppression weakens structure from within."

Desire leads to "silence body of an image."

One floats in the small compressions to "all of them each of them revelations of objectivity (a subject) / gatelessness a roof in the air."

Gatelessness/erotic love does (would) not give credibility to or have longing for 'masculine' 'tradition', to one's being borrowed, or not being so. Credibility to, or connections of, comparisons is the fake origin.

To 'analyze' itself is the fake origin.

Gatelessness causes being "in lovely blue" to arise. A radical state of love is falsified by my hypothesis.

What's modern is the writing being to state structure in order to see 'objectively' *its* reverberation solely. The placing of statements beside each other arises from the inner (individual) being constantly stated incorrectly by 'Authority' and (so) by the inner individual oneself as well.

Continually resembled by oneself even, one continues to reform structure (of writing and of outside) to be ahead of reality because "the city is unrecognizable" (*Saturn*).

The base of examination of actual military war is the mirror of writing-structure now "The crucial / tension the war is not separate from us."

Structure (not 'representing') disallows separation intensely in "transgressive responsibility" by being continually separate from reality.

There is allowed the young child sucked up inside the vacuum cleaner and blown back out lying dead, some other person. 'Structure' opens infinitely now to see the unknown world.

Nicheless Comparisons

Jean Day's writing is on two straddling lines in *The I and the You*, as double comparison to a missing referent. The two 'blind' sides refer to (are) a (missing) concurrence.

Dropping it in the center, feeling takes place at the ends, where it appears not to be a ground of comparison.

It's a ground by being dropped.

The missing referent is not grounds for beauty, so beauty occurs in the concurrence of these. By not being the standard, the accepted which is "Elaborate and just, the words of concurrence / realized as beauty," that line is serious and real.

Both of the comparisons (throughout) are rational schemata being referent to the senses outside us. The dual illuminates a trajectory that is not its schemata.

It is a double negative which has a light trajectory.

It's never dropped which occurs by dropping itself. That's two.

The grounds of comparison separately drop: "Both rational in inference and evident / to the senses outside ourselves."

There's no basis for opinion of an individual (for knowledge) except on one's (our) own reflection. "And deep and I continue with a snack / for the nonexistent is neither something nor suchlike."

So translation occurs on one strand (line) where brilliance carries over (on) the lines of both. They're illuminating nonexistence ("in dreaming, her brilliance carries over / indexically").

The grounds of comparison flood the line. Where there's the single strand only, it floods because "No words equal music."

This fills in the missing concurrence without a belief system. The comparisons are equal, similar, narrowed to flood: "Skinheads VS. / a disturbance."

The two separate lines being the comparison, that is to nature ("sets the night of nature"), and to us ("like night on the brain of the living"), two dissimilarities. So comparison itself is united because it's similar.

"As in nature, we are richeless and can't compare with frogs."

Love is continual dual (mutual) scepticism that isolates it from social hype, occurs free.

The comparison is "romantic / in its rejection of romance."

Erotic becomes the relations of structure therefore, only, is made to be seen as that.

As the subjective union is the grounds of comparison, where there's no comparison, the present is flooded, everything brought to it, as to one line where there's no negative space.

But it got there by negative space.

The completely simple present where everything is " 'leaks' back into the crowd." That ordinary life where the bodhisattvas stand is the concurrence arrived at by the series of eliminations which are the effect of 'groundless' comparisons.

We are in it there, the line.

Writing on Rim

This entire essay is an experiment as comparisons, my intention being not to make them concur either before as a hypothesis, or while observing them. Yet my observing *is* concurrence as the comparisons as such. The following section of the essay was begun on request for an issue of *Conjunctions*. Part was published there.

Dimly had seen the stiff orange brush lacquered standing up on the white frame riding on the sheet. When there'd been a slash in the side the orange halo rising above and film of white skin on the bikes in the fume. It rides away flickering in the fume. The back of his head gradually flickering.

She sees him for the first time as a memory later, in reverse to him having flickered.

bowing to that.

The bike riding in heavy grass. The roar of it riding in the heavy hemp. Bike up dirt slope entirely separate from it. In air whirring. She is not there or seeing it.

He's making a delivery. Puts out some white powder on the table.

As if his teeth are hollow or he's translucent. So that feeling animates him rather than him being able.

The soft brush of red grass is around the inlet. Being able isn't there.

It's from the inside. And then with a switchblade he makes a cut in the man at the table. That's flat then.

Swan flapping flying above hennaed field does not appear to move after passing it (the swan). Its joy, which is from this seeing it, would have been from itself — from this. It can see itself there. — from Defoe

The germ of *Defoe* was war, the rising fear and inner resistance preceding the bombing of Iraq, intertwined with memories 'leaking out' from the Vietnam War period, and then from all periods of one's/my subjective field — as if that is a visual field that is opened and at the same time narrowed to its sky horizon (as the entire rim of the actual sky) as concentration.

So that the night and all actual dreams, whatever were occurring then, abut the day, are in it — and the rim of that (form) actual horizon is held and eliminated, as concentration.

72

Voices giving accounts are woven in the text as history which is just an academic category.

The real landscape is flattened as a disc by fictionalizing and is placed against other discs floating.

Epic is bathos made possible by movement.

The real moon is made to abut the fictional landscape. The landscape is bounced off actual (horizon) rim, in that what's realistic is narrowed and abutted to what's realistic. It scrutinizes by eliminating itself (disc) narrowing it to the rim.

Fictionalizing is then the inner mind. War is that. And also utter freedom. Ordinary sleeping dreams, which were my actual events, were taken into those days (which followed the dreams) and became even with them, abutted them as their occurrence. A disc of still day occurred really, in which the fictionalized movement flickered.

One can see the disc of a day floating and the disc of the actual day-moon in it by separating them and fictionalizing.

It does not create either.

It could be seen by it's being smashed or calm.

Epic occurs fragile from one's interior movements. There are masses of people moving in front of it. The delicate yellow cord of one's spine doesn't produce.

Epic is floated in front of documentaries. It is based in fulfilling community. There isn't community any more.

In so far as I noticed myself trying to change or avert reality by the writing, I had to recognize that motive, note where it's occurring, which is fantasy.

Rather, the writing should be pushed to be itself only concentration — in which is one's fear, anger, etc.

Anger and distortions of clarity are of the nature of perceiving that reality. It can't be seen otherwise.

The text eliminates subjective grounds.

There's extreme pain without it.

One has to be fragile to be without protection in this reality. This eliminates the separation between writing and realistic rim.

Also to push 'it' to where even weariness causes it (no difference between weariness and the horizon and writing) to collapse on itself where it's still, visibly flapping.

I wanted to get the writing to the point of being that still. "A memory as just a thin disc, as it is seen that way. there is no event. Warm, the birds stirring and flying. I had a memory of being on an empty street in San Diego near by the ocean, just that. that as a disc because it became so stagnant it seemed it was going to collapse, and be still. it flapped. my mind had become so tired its resistance was going. The mind being weary as clarifying in itself."

We see actual phenomena unconsciously. Phenomena are interpreted before they appear. In *Defoe* sheets of images of action float up.

The current culture is produced in one as one's inner self. One is fluently seeing it and producing its/oneself images.

Epics occur before documentaries. They are in reverse and inside. Aeneas has to be not accepted as the leader.

(Thus the subjective ground is eliminated which created documentaries.)

The placement in space of the figures (hurling above each other in battle or being inside an out-stretched figure running) is constructed and imagined like the translation of psyche in the space of our ads, action movies which are our meeting with experience here, or Renaissance paintings; a structure duplicating the history of itself, it's seeing. The culture being in one separates it. As such it's inside, super-real.

Negative space is the most rigorous scrutiny in this culture. This blasts images up out of it that float there.

Rigor as apprehension of reality has to be 'seen' to be an illusion, of itself.

The form of rigor itself has to undercut its concept ('masculine' 'tradition' that there is a form of rigor which is the basis of apprehension). One is not to have a ground or basis of apprehension or it's inaccurate — even this concept of not having a basis, and see where this emerges.

Revery of struggle is not a basis.

Images of struggle in the text (battle in which figures seen by the viewer float over each other slashing or whirling, a construct fictionalizing) are the occurrence itself 'without' rigor.

The form is the occurrence.

Seeing events as bathos and ridiculing them, light thought is compared to the horizon. It straddles it without uniting ever.

When it doesn't unite it's very strong (once one's juxtaposing to the rim). That's subtracting what's human from it (rim).

There is only modern. We're stranded here (which is fine), separated from conceptualizing so images are arising from that.

Writing can only give a sense of where not conceptualizing occurs.

The constructed imagined space is a kind of blank where one is not conceptualizing.

Defoe is in two parts, "Part I: Waking Life" and "Part II: Defoe." Amongst the streams of sort of pop plots in "Waking Life": 'the (other)' who is the main figure, in love with James Dean as he is not as an image, is at one point on a desert which is exploding with fires in which the henna man, a drugdealer, wrapped in a cocoon is carried by starving boys.

Inner life is the same as epic, as fantasy, super-real. Or ego. Their separation has been eliminated. So they are real.

Images arise as the way of undercutting the image in one: because they do not resemble themselves or war. So these images float out, as the bulb of the sun does, eliminated on the rim (which vastly actually physically expands — as the form, frame):

75

One just sees from one's social group perspective say and then the huge bright day is dilated flapping with that; so it's involuntarily let go as it's large and while hitting the recesses in front of one in the present, remains there shuttering.

If it doesn't unite with the horizon it's not suffering. Then sometime it unites peacefully.

In fact, one here has to be torn apart by other cultures cleaving to them at the same time as to one's own. Seeing that's unnecessary now is one being eliminated on the rim also, peacefully.

Relations between people are not sustained by anything.

Being depressed is dropping a stick that falls in deep water without anything around it. Nothing sustains it. It isn't oneself floating.

Writing is not being sustained also. The writing has to have nothing sustaining it. To find that place is duration.

That is current time. We aren't sustained and fulfill community. For no reason.

In "Part II: Defoe," a character emerges a woman named Defoe. The form of the writing is to be utter simplicity so that while personality emerges its movements arise and are seen from not having self-confidence.

The text has to make the social life be brought to only going on as the effect of (perceiving without self-confidence) or after that.

One has to stop doing the social actions. At all.

One's to bring action to the delicate, yellow cord in one's spine. How?

Plot is so simple in Part II that it has nothing to do with reflecting social or private psyche, which it is. It can't generate it.

What is the simplest motion possible?

All actions are bathos, so one can utterly relax. A space is created by duration in which all actions are responsive to each other, in fact.

Fictionalizing is the most reciprocal and realistic quintessence. Disruption is in relation to it peacefully.

That is the life eliminated to the rim, on which actions float off.

It objectifies real phenomena. One's rim (history) that is the present is brought onto one frame on which actions don't disappear. They all appear there.

It's one's actual death eliminated (narrowed) to be life. We don't see one's death here.

We have to take it past that.

The 'finished work' is a hypothesis to be dropped. I'm trying to have the work (which may not be there yet in the book) occur as 'essay' now.

There is a great difference between Part I and Part II as if they are separate 'books'. An intellectual leap takes place (that is when one does not know something) in the space between the two parts. It is not in content that follows it.

Whereas in Part I the real present is the writing and one is small in it, in Part II the minute historical event of the real past takes place in the writing's structure: one of the first labor strikes in Japan, that of fourteen to sixteen year-old girls living in a factory, occurs in the present.

The real event is evanescent on plot as the first time.

A structure is realistic and enlarged widely on real minute event. The structures of these two parts (and there being a separation between them) do not, are not to, theorize connections, while being that — that is what structure *is*.

It's not ever known. Is not in behavior. Not being a subject. Events don't occur from anything. They're the same as structure, in existence. An extension of space occurs from there not being juxtaposition to or imitation of the real event while it

77

appears to occur. An intellectual leap is not produced from plot nor is event. It doesn't occur anywhere in what follows it, isn't before it.

An intellectual leap: it's structure as observation. It's simple (that's *when* it occurs), which isn't in any part of the book, *Defoe*.

Positions of erotica occur in the text, which are love then. In those exact minute motions; these have a rhythm of presentation in the text that is in spurts and not planned. When it is subject to only its movement, it has no other reflection. It isn't social perception; or rather, is it *only* then. What's that?

One separates on the rim, straddling.

Narrowing the rim to 'masculine' from oneself (if one's a woman) is being one alone.

That's produced by people.

'Masculine' being brought to, narrowed to oneself (if one's a woman) is the rim belying its social perception.

So it's belying the entire construction.

The event (disc) is the occurrence. The form is the occurrence.

They're at the rim washing together.

Events have their own movement washing in it.

One's 'masculine' 'tradition' say.

One's own movement touches the rim and floats off of it. Narrowing is for clarity, but it's everywhere. Writing has to get past social reflection; dawn's on dusk.

Empathy, Mei-mei Berssenbrugge, Station Hill Press,
 Annandale-on-Hudson, 1989
Sphericity, Mei-mei Berssenbrugge, Kelsey St. Press,
 Berkeley, 1993
Metamorphopsia, Norma Cole, Potes & Poets Press,
 Elmwood, 1988
from *Saturn*, Norma Cole, in *War*, O Books, Oakland, 1991
The I and the You, Jean Day, Potes & Poets Press,
 Elmwood, 1993
The Words, Carla Harryman, manuscript in progress, 1993
Oxota: A Short Russian Novel, Lyn Hejinian, The Figures Press,
 Gt. Barrington, 1991
The Cell, Lyn Hejinian, Sun & Moon Press, Los Angeles, 1993
Better Hearing Behind Walls, Erica Hunt, Roof Press,
 New York, 1993
Rondeaux, Laura Moriarty, Roof Press, New York, 1990
Defoe, Leslie Scalapino, Sun & Moon, Los Angeles, 1994

OTHER ROOF BOOKS

Andrews, Bruce. **Getting Ready To Have Been Frightened**. 116p. $7.50.

Andrews, Bruce. **R & B**. 32p. $2.50.

Bee, Susan [Laufer]. **The Occurrence of Tune**, text by Charles Bernstein. 9 plates, 24p. $6.

Benson, Steve. **Blue Book**. Copub. with The Figures. 250p. $12.50

Bernstein, Charles. **Controlling Interests**. 88p. $6.

Bernstein, Charles. **Islets/Irritations**. 112p. $9.95.

Bernstein, Charles (editor). **The Politics of Poetic Form**. 246p. $12.95; cloth $21.95.

Brossard, Nicole. **Picture Theory**. 188p. $11.95.

Child, Abigail. **From Solids**. 30p. $3.

Davies, Alan. **Active 24 Hours**. 100p. $5.

Davies, Alan. **Signage**. 184p. $11.

Davies, Alan. **Rave**. 80p. $9.95.

Day, Jean. **A Young Recruit**. 58p. $6.

Dickenson, George-Thérèse. **Transducing**. 175p. $7.50.

Di Palma, Ray. **Raik**. 100p. $9.95.

Dreyer, Lynne. **The White Museum**. 80p. $6.

Edwards, Ken. **Good Science**. 80p. $9.95.

Eigner, Larry. **Areas Lights Heights**. 182p. $12, $22 (cloth).

Estrin, Jerry. **Rome, A Mobile Home**. Copub. with The Figures, O Books, and Potes & Poets. 88p. $9.95.

Gizzi, Michael. **Continental Harmonies**. 92p. $8.95.

Gottlieb, Michael. **Ninety-Six Tears**. 88p. $5.

Grenier, Robert. **A Day at the Beach**. 80p. $6.

Hills, Henry. **Making Money**. 72p. $7.50. VHS videotape $24.95.
   Book & tape $29.95.

Hunt, Erica. **Local History**. 80 p. $9.95.

Inman, P. **Red Shift**. 64p. $6.

Lazer, Hank. **Doublespace**. 192 p. $12.

Legend. Collaboration by Andrews, Bernstein, DiPalma, McCaffery, and Silliman.
   Copub. with L=A=N=G=U=A=G=E. 250p. $12.

Mac Low, Jackson. **Representative Works: 1938–1985**. 360p. $12.95, $18.95 (cloth).

Mac Low, Jackson. **Twenties**. 112p. $8.95.

McCaffery, Steve. **North of Intention**. 240p. $12.95.

Moriarty, Laura. **Rondeaux**. 107p. $8.

Neilson, Melanie. **Civil Noir**. 96p. $8.95.

Pearson, Ted. **Planetary Gear**. 72p. $8.95.

Perelman, Bob. **Face Value**. 72p. $6.

Perelman, Bob. **Virtual Reality**. 80p. $9.95.

Piombino, Nick, **The Boundary of Blur**. 128p. $13.95

Robinson, Kit. **Balance Sheet**. 112 p. $9.95.

Robinson, Kit. **Ice Cubes**. 96p. $6.

Scalapino, Leslie. **Objects in the Terrifying Tense Longing from Taking Place**. 88p. $9.95.

Seaton, Peter. **The Son Master**. 64p. $4.

Sherry, James. **Popular Fiction**. 84p. $6.

Silliman, Ron. **The New Sentence**. 200p. $10.

Templeton, Fiona. **YOU—The City**. 150p. $11.95.

Ward, Diane. **Relation**. 64p. $7.50.

Watten, Barrett. **Progress**. 122p. $7.50.

Weiner, Hannah. **Little Books/Indians**. 92p. $4.

For ordering or complete catalog write:
SEGUE FOUNDATION, ROOF BOOKS, 303 East 8th Street, New York, NY 10009